Series Editor: MEIC STEPHENS

Stage Welsh

Nation, nationalism and theatre: the search for cultural identity

David Adams

First Impression—October 1996

ISBN 1 85902 344 4

Printed in Wales at
Gomer Press, Llandysul, Ceredigion

PROLOGUE

It's back: The Great Welsh National Theatre Debate

We had it with Lloyd George, we had it around the time of the First World War, we had it in the troublesome Thirties, we had it in the radical Sixties. Now in the postmodernist Nineties as the Millennium approaches, the issue is on the table again. The Welsh theatre world is divided. The public, probably, couldn't care less.

The most unlikely, as well as the predictable, personalities have joined the debate. But supporters have always seemed strange bedfellows. Today it's Michael Bogdanov, Welsh theatre director, socialist, populariser, and until recently Julian Mitchell, English playwright, rightwing liberal, elitist. But George Bernard Shaw, Lord Howard de Walden, Harley Granville Barker, Lloyd George, Saunders Lewis and Richard Burton have all at some time called for a Welsh National Theatre.

Because the Great National Theatre Debate is really about more than theatre. It is about the state of Wales, about cultural identity, about nationalism and internationalism. But the debaters talk only about theatre.

Michael Bogdanov, with homes near Brecon and now in Cardiff Bay, where he has just directed a film version of *The Tempest*, and Julian Mitchell, fresh from his success as one of the writers of *Inspector Morse*, opera adaptations and filmscripts, briefly joined forces a few years ago when it was expected that there would be a new Labour government with a Welsh prime minister and a national assembly for Wales. Bogdanov, as a returning émigré Welshman, and Mitchell, as Chairman of the Welsh Arts Council's Drama Committee, shared a belief in the unrealised potential of Welsh theatre and wanted to see a major production company serving the whole country; they now seem to have gone their different ways.

Julian Mitchell believed that a National Theatre should be based on Theatr Clwyd touring around the country from its North Wales base. Bogdanov's recent revival of the campaign was launched with a speech celebrating his Honorary Professorship at the University of Wales and with a manifesto in *The Guardian* a few days later where he bemoaned the "scandal" of the failure to establish a National Theatre of Wales and suggested such a company could be based at the proposed Cardiff Bay Opera House. Phil Clark, the Director of the Sherman Theatre and a committed supporter of community theatre, joined Bogdanov's campaign. Neil Kinnock and Dafydd Elis Thomas jumped on the bandwagon, though not necessarily in any particular brigade. The London-based scourge of Arts Council policies and self-publicist Dedwydd Jones re-entered the arena. A meeting hosted by BBC Controller Geraint Talfan Davies was snubbed by the great and the good who were invited and condemned by theatre practitioners, who weren't, but Bogdanov and Clark persevered. A new consultation document was circulated and they claimed the support of the Arts Council of Wales, BBC, HTV and WDA. Now an embryonic National Theatre Trust is lobbying for an ambitious plan based on the German federal system, with a new purpose-built theatre and a Welsh National Theatre Company to be resident there (prop. M. Bogdanov, presumably). It may be possible, even, that its home would be Mold, where at the time of writing Theatr Clwyd's future still seems uncertain.

Various obvious problems leap out. With no tradition of mainstage production, where will the writers and directors come from; with arts funding tighter than ever, where will the huge ongoing costs come from; and with a relatively small potential audience, where will the punters come from? The supporters claim that expats (like Bogdanov, Anthony Hopkins, Jonathan Pryce, Sean Matthias and..er...) will flock back, that the Lottery will cough up a few millions and that tourists (Cardiff's projected growth industry) will make up the majority of the audience. Pass the salt. Wales is a small country, a lot smaller in population than

Yorkshire, say, and its capital city, Cardiff, is a little bigger than Kingston-upon-Hull and is smaller than Doncaster; in European terms, Cardiff is about the same size as the capital cities of Albania and Slovenia. The amount of theatrical activity in Wales may be already out of all proportion to the population - but nearly half the population of Wales do go to the theatre at least once a year. The Bogdanov campaign is wrong when it claims that theatre has failed to find an audience in Wales - it's just that the optimum audience is relatively small.

The latest Great National Theatre Debate comes, ironically, as theatre in England is in a parlous state. Centuries' worth of development - from the religious dramas of the Dark Ages through medieval miracle plays to the Jacobethan flowering of Shakespeare and his contemporaries, from the rebuilding of the tradition after the Restoration to the elegant wit of the eighteenth century and from the social consciences of the Edwardians to the kitchen-sink dramas of the Fifties and the pluralist mainstream work of today - all looks set to crumble within a decade as the cornerstone of English theatre, the building-based so-called "rep" company, all but disappears. The fifty or so building-based companies throughout England, who train and employ actors, directors, designers and technicians and present the work of living dramatists as well as dead ones, could be replaced by a mere dozen "supercompanies" who will doubtless recycle the same twenty or so "classics". English theatre looks sick.

Theatre in Wales is, by comparison, very healthy. The day after Michael Bogdanov's *Guardian* article, for example, I listened to Powys-based playwright Greg Cullen's poetic, political, marvellous *Tower*, produced in Cardiff, broadcast on Radio 4. That week Swansea-based Volcano Theatre's deconstruction of Ibsen, *How To Live*, was at Waterman's in London. Made in Wales was staging its eight-week *Trouble and Desire* festival of new writing at The Point in Cardiff Bay. Ed Thomas's startling, brilliantly-made exploration of an imagined Wales, *Song for a Forgotten City*, for Y Cwmni, was touring to Aberystwyth and Builth Wells before going to The Royal Court.

Another, new, physical theatre company from Swansea, Frantic Theatre, was giving Osborne a going-over with their version of *Look Back in Anger* and opening their latest energetic reworking, *Volpone*, at Taliesin Arts Centre. Dalier Sylw launched the tour of their rugby-set satire, *Y Cinio (The Dinner)*, at Cardiff Arms Park to coincide with the Wales-Ireland women's international. The Sherman Theatre's season of lunch-time theatre produced in co-operation with HTV continued, as did the 22-event *Independent Dance Festival* at Chapter Arts Centre. The week before, Brith Gof's *Y Pen Bas/Y Pen Dwfn* made riveting television on S4C. All over Wales community groups were performing in village halls and schools. More conventionally, The Sherman Theatre Company were touring *Romeo and Juliet*, Theatr Gwynedd's Welsh and English versions of Kitchener Davies's *Cwm Glo* hit Cardiff and Theatr Clwyd had opened *Mrs Warren's Profession* in Mold prior to a tour. With few exceptions, new, innovatory, different, Welsh or Welsh-flavoured and all despite the "scandal" of the failure to create a National Theatre.

As an outside insider, an English critic of Welsh theatre, I offer some observations.

Nation

Nationalism, nationhood and cultural identity are slippery concepts and ones of which I wouldn't want to pretend to have a confident grasp; others with a greater knowledge and interest have explored them in this *Changing Wales* series. But as a documentor and critic of theatre in Wales for over 15 years, I am faced again with the idea of a National Theatre of Wales. And so nation, nationalism and nationhood, culture and identity, language and race, all demand attention along with the artistic, economic and ideological questions of theatre itself. I stress here that in the pages that follow I do not pretend to present a cohesive, prescriptive argument for or against a National Theatre: I think many of us these days are a little wary of the all-embracing, deterministic, linear, narrative argument. Instead, I offer a personal range of lateral perspectives.

I think we need to start by considering our terms. I have subtitled this essay "Nation, Nationalism and Theatre: the Search for Cultural Identity" and what I want to explore is far more than the pros and cons of a National Theatre of Wales. The concept raises a range of issues about culture and the role of theatre within a culture at a time when Wales as a nation (accepting the word *pro tem*) seems to be on the verge of being accepted in its own right and Welsh theatre, possibly the youngest in Europe, is at an exciting stage of development as it too enters maturity. I will lay my cards on the table now and state that for many years I have found the idea of a National Theatre of Wales at best redundant and a distraction; today, perhaps, the situation has changed. But in exploring the implications I believe we can touch on a multitude of concerns in a changing world.

Now part of the case for a National Theatre is that a nation needs institutions to legitimize itself: that is why a National Assembly is seen as crucial and the replacement of Welsh law by the Tudors was so damaging. But not all such "national" institutions do that. Just how much, for example, does the Welsh National Opera say anything about Wales? Peter Lord's critiques (including his admirable essay in this series) have demanded that the National Museum should address itself to its hitherto ignored cultural role. Could a National Theatre be a vital element in the defining of Welsh identity?

First, we need to confront the National part of this National Theatre of Wales. What a difference a capital letter makes! Wales already has a national theatre, in the sense of "national" meaning "nationwide" (and "theatre" meaning the practice rather than a building). National, with a capital N, is a word that is resonant with meaning: National Anthem, National Front, National Health, National Eisteddfod, National Socialism. Is nationalism the same as nation-ism? Is a nation simply "an imagined community"? Does nationalism mean excluding non-nationals?

The name Wales, as we all know, comes from *wealas*, the Anglo-Saxon word for "foreign": Wales is only Wales to those who do not live there, an immensely significant point. To those who do, they are *Cymry*, "compatriots", hence *Cymru*. It is, then, a country nominally, literally, defined by whether you live there or not.

But, as Professor Gwyn Alf Williams asked, When was Wales? The Romans, whose records are the earliest we have, wrote about the tribes who occupied this western peninsula of Britain (or Prydain). There were the Silures, who inhabited a land that on the east had a dense wood of which the Forest of Dean is the remnant; the Cornovii, whose territory was to the north of the Silures; the Ordovices, to the west of the Silures; in the far north, the Deceangli; in the far west, the Demetae. (If you are Welsh, from which of these five tribes do you come?) By the end of the eighth century, when Offa ruled neighbouring Mercia, West Britain had a distinct north and south: in the north, Gwynedd and Powys, in the south Morgannwg, the old land of the Silures, and Deheubarth, which grew out of Dyfed; to reinforce the complexity of the situation, we understand that the north was enmeshed with the Saxons and the south and west were settled extensively by Irish immigrants. Offa's famous Dyke (apparently built around 790, although it is totally appropriate there is no record of its construction: it is just *there*) was probably a negotiated boundary but a division that has passed into common usage (at least on the English side) as a definition of Welsh or English. Perhaps by 927, when Athelstan met Hywel Dda and the lesser Welsh kings on the banks of the Wye and made them an offer they couldn't refuse, Wales as a nation was properly established, albeit as one subservient to England. By 1282, when Edward defeated Llywelyn, the Last of the Princes, and formally annexed the land of Wales to England, defining its inhabitants as "mere Welshmen", the nation ironically had a real identity - as a colony. And since 1410 and the defeat of Glyndwr's rebellion Wales may quite certainly have been a nation - a nation defined to some extent by its lack of independence. The 1536 Act of Union merely confirmed its status as an annexe of England.

Where do I stand? On the outside, looking in. Just.

I was born in the Forest of Dean, and my family tree, energetically researched, as it happens, by a Welsh cousin, goes back only 500 years. I am a product of the land of the Silures and, but for Offa's Dyke, a symbolic rather than practical wall which divided the land of the Silures more than the River Wye ever seemed to, I might be Welsh. (Should I mention now that the great Welsh rugby team of 1905 that defeated the All Blacks, in an event that was seen by many to have been the birth of the new Welsh nation, was captained by a centre-threequarter, Gwyn Nicholls, from the Forest of Dean? Or that I was even born in a town, Lydney, that conceivably took its name from Lludd, the great Celtic god and Welsh mythical hero?) Maybe if Aethelfrith's Chester-Gloucester boundary of 616 had been stuck to, I might be as much of a *Cymro* as my hypothetical ancestor would have then so deemed. Or if my grandparents had stayed in the Rhondda, to whence they temporarily removed during the First World War, I would be at least as Welsh as my cousin. However, I am about five miles away from qualification thanks to Offa and his boundary and despite coming from a family of coalminers, chapelgoers and singers, and having Roberts as a family name just one generation back, despite my father's forenames being Ivon Idris, I am unlike my cousins not by any definition Welsh: I do not speak Welsh, I do not come from a culture created as much as anything by the oppression of a dominant neighbour, I am certainly less Welsh than many in South Wales who call themselves Gudjerati, Somali, Chinese, Afro-Caribbean, Irish or Italian but whose families have been in Wales for generations.

I should say, though, that I am not immune from feelings of belonging to a place. I do recognize the importance of roots and what we might call a "cultural consciousness", a sense of belonging, *y filltir sgwar*: I feel it for the Forest of Dean, but not for England or Britain, and so am dubious about the notion of patriotism as well as nationalism. And, yes, I am suspicious of those who proclaim in a patriotic way for Wales rather than an immediate geographic area with which they might understandably associate. I suspect that when someone from The Rhondda, for example, calls themself Welsh, they really mean they're from Rhondda Fawr, or rather Treherbert, because any Welsh street can by easy synecdoche become Wales. What is Wales? Welsh Wales, cosmopolitan South Wales, *Y Gogledd, Y Fro Gymraeg*, the people of Little England Beyond Wales, the Gwentians who passionately think of themselves as English, the Cardis - all are in many ways separate and only in the last thirty years or so has the increase in Welsh learners and Welsh television tended to homogenize the Welsh language and minimize regional colloquialism. Do they all make up a nation, a coherent whole enough to have a nationalist policy? Crucially, if we accept (and surely we do) that not only will Welsh never again be the majority language of Wales but also that Wales, unlike other British colonies or ex-Soviet satellites, will always be part of a larger Britain, what meaning does the status of "nation" have? And if there is a sense of nationhood, how would this be expressed through the medium of theatre?

Personally, I have no interest in the nationalism question. I inhabit a multicultural world and I see nationalism too often as a synonym for racism or a convenient call to defend the values of a dominant ideology, as when John Major twisted Orwell to evoke a sub-Shakespearean Britain of cricket, warm beer and tea as a metaphor for the preservation of a conservative, white, patriarchal, capitalist, anaesthetized way of life. But I do think that the search for a cultural identity in Wales in the last twenty years has contributed to a distinctively exciting, innovative theatre that is a telling contrast to the arid, boring theatre that symbolizes England's decline over the same period. Welsh theatre is worthy of celebration as it matures into a significant force and a strong voice in a new Europe.

I ask only: Is it not heterogeneity rather than homogeneity that defines this cultural identity? Is this cultural identity the same as nationalism? And does institutionalising it by inventing a National Theatre of Wales diminish or enhance the value of it?

And I raise here the philosophical question that is at the very root of not just this brief enquiry but of all art: what is cultural identity - does it have any real meaning, is it merely an ideological construct, is it a motivating force or an unattainable ideal ? I offer you this succinct summary of the problem from Marcia Tucker: "The problem of identity - personal, cultural, social, sexual and racial - is one of the most vexing critical issues of our time. The mythical notion that there is a single identity discoverable 'within' a particular individual or group has been replaced in recent years by the growing understanding that fixed identities are the product of the far from disinterested ways in which we are represented to ourselves and to others."

We need, then, to challenge the myth of a cohesive "cultural identity" just as much as "nationalism" and to ask how, why and in whose interests it was created.

Culture

The questions of language, culture, colonialism and race are, especially in a bilingual country, inextricably linked to the problems of nationalism and national identity. Nationalism seems in general to be about keeping a culture for the inhabitants of a particular country; internationalism, the sharing of cultures, I find far more attractive (but then, you might say, I would, wouldn't I, as someone whose national tongue and identity has never been under threat). As Westerners we may all be aware of the dangers of becoming "cultural tourists" when we appropriate Bhundu Boys music or Indian food or Tibetan rugs; we take what we want from an exotic culture, selecting from a position of dominant power. It is a thin line between this and appreciating, sharing and respecting another culture and as an English person writing about Welsh culture I have to admit this difficulty. But if theatre is a crucible of civilizations, as Victor Hugo said, a place for human communication, then to find out about Welsh culture, to share what it has to say, I go to the theatre.

Now if I see that theatre in the Welsh language I know it is probably (although there are Welsh-language works that are very English) a Welsh cultural product. But I can also see in Wales theatre in the English language and I might wonder: is this culturally Welsh or culturally English? There are many (R. S. Thomas, for one) who assert that Welsh work in English cannot be considered Welsh and contributes only to English culture. So is language a defining characteristic of cultural product? And is there a difference between Welsh theatre in Welsh and Welsh theatre in English? It is not a problem confined to Wales (or to theatre), but Wales is different in that the native language is spoken by a minority (and solely by a very small minority, if at all: only one percent were monoglot Welsh twenty-five years ago, statistically none today). Despite the small audience Welsh-language theatre is clearly lively and popular - but also sometimes exclusive, with no desire to share its content with non-Welsh speakers. I have been at the theatre in Wales when I have very much felt an unwelcome outsider, someone whose Englishness meant they might want to expropriate the play in the same way as many wanted to buy a home - a settler, a colonizer of the cultural product as well as the land. But is not exclusivity racist?

Now is this hypothetical National Theatre of Wales international or intranational? In other words, does it look outwards or inwards? For many people, I suggest, the extent to which Welsh theatre can represent a discrete Welsh culture if it is not in the Welsh language is today less of an issue. There is more to theatre than language, for a start, and the first language of theatre is the *lingua franca* of performance. Of course by speaking in English, the language of a dominant power but also the most widely understood language of western culture, theatre immediately does become to some extent *inter*cultural. Work in Welsh is by its very nature *intra*cultural, speaking to or about a small minority, and it is arguable whether it is an essential expression of cultural independence. There are several issues here, and to an extent they are remarkably similar to questions of cultural identity faced by other post-colonial nations, from the USA to former USSR states by way of Australia, New Zealand, Canada, India, Kenya, Nigeria, Algeria, Central America and so on - countries which often had a language imposed on them, and with it a cultural domination, and who then faced, with their political independence, the challenge of in some cases both recovering their native language and using the imposed language to define a sense of cultural identity. And by "language" we should also mean "expressive medium" - such as theatre, which is a mixture of form and speech. Critical theorists would use the term "discourse".

What post-colonial cultures have found is that it is simply not possible to "indigenize" the dominant form - in other words, you cannot transpose without radical alteration an English form to somewhere else that merely shares the same language and some customs and traditions. American literature has developed a distinctive voice despite being in the English language - but it did so only after trying and failing to copy English fiction genres.

More immediately, for example, Alan Ayckbourn's style of comedy, it seems to me, cannot (despite being in the dominant language) be translated to Wales, unless that Wales is the very Anglicized middle-class Wales that is really not culturally Wales, because the plays are about specific locations and a specific culture and are culturally English. For Welsh theatre to lay claim to being part of a Welsh culture it has to reject English theatrical forms.

But if plays are in English, are they not part of the same common tradition, branches of the same tree? This is where the bizarre label "Anglo-Welsh" comes from, with the suggestion that Welsh writers employing the English language are part of the common English literary heritage. Tell Ed Thomas or Ian Rowlands that they are "Anglo-Welsh"! It is surely time we abandoned this patronizing sobriquet. We don't call Albert Camus Franco-Algerian or Wole Soyinka Anglo-Nigerian. Enough Welsh writers, in fiction, poetry and drama, have shown that English (or "english" as the language of Jamaican, Australian, Kenyan, etc. writers has been labelled, to differentiate the speech from the expression of colonial power) can be appropriated and used in a non-English way, turning the language back on itself by using it to express opposition to Englishness. There is still, for sure, the Welsh writer who uses English, deliberately or unconsciously, to express their adoption and absorption into a centralized, "British" culture - a literary *Dic Sion Dafydd* who turns their back on their indigenous culture without ever necessarily having to cross the Severn Bridge. But we can see Dylan Thomas or Caradoc Evans's linguistic excesses as attempts to employ an imported language to express a sense of difference, an awareness of being on the periphery, at the margins of a centralized culture. Ed Thomas and Ian Rowlands do the same. It is perfectly possible to produce Welsh work in English (or "english") that has quite different characteristics from English-language work produced by English writers and so can be considered the product of another discrete culture. For proof, look at the USA, Australia, New Zealand and Canada.

It is also the case that anti-French Algerian and Moroccan writers, for example, deliberately write in French as well as their native tongue. Edward Said, the Palestinian critic who urges us to re-read Western texts from a colonial perspective, points out that the challenge for writers in colonized cultures is to use the language of their oppressors to talk about their own culture from their point of view rather than let English writers offer their inevitable (colonial) view. Said extends his theory of "orientalism" - he says that the Orient was an invention of the West to exercise power and justify their imperial ambitions - to all kinds of colonized and oppressed peoples and I shall explore its application to Wales presently. His views are remarkably similar to Gwyn Alf's: he too talks of the need to reinvent oneself but Said, like Welsh critic Raymond Williams, is more concerned with geography than history. One of the best plays to come out of Wales, incidentally, tackles precisely this issue: Greg Cullen's *Frida and Diego* is about two committed socialist Mexican artists who deliberately subverted American capitalist culture to criticise it - the highpoint of Diego Rivera's mural painting is the huge public work in Detroit commissioned by Ford that graphically expresses the oppression of workers under the capitalist system. The playwright's intended very relevant metaphor for the Welsh situation was ironically missed, even by Made in Wales Stage Company, who rejected the play because it wasn't "Welsh" enough! (*Frida and Diego* was first staged to great critical acclaim by Red Shift and was eventually produced in Wales under the writer's direction by Mid Powys Youth Theatre.)

The post-colonial argument is problematic in Wales, of course. First, most post-colonial nations would question Wales's claim to be included in the argument at all - on the grounds that Wales allegedly not only willingly submitted to colonization by Tudor England but was complicit in British colonialism abroad. And crucially, Wales has not become independent - and maybe never will, at least in the sense that other former colonies have gained political and cultural independence. We may question what "decolonization" means but it is unlikely, to say the least, that English will ever be seen as a passing historical feature in Wales; the English language is overwhelmingly that of the majority and aspects of the English culture would be difficult to uproot. A more realistic attitude is that cultural syncrecity is not only inevitable but can actually be valuable and a source of specific strength.

If the native tongue, then, is not a defining characteristic of cultural identity, and the Welshness of Welsh theatre, what is? It must be the awareness of the colonized as being different from the colonizers. In Welsh theatre I can see some appropriations from English culture (a kind of reverse colonialization) but several manifestations of a different cultural identity, most of which are not survivors of bygone days but newly-formed. It is, actually, again a phenomenon noted in post-colonial cultures - for those on the "margins" as it were, alienated by the process of colonisation, their position could be turned into a very positive one where they were forced through a kind of mental barrier and were able to see their experiences as uncentred (or "ex-centric" to use the jargon), pluralistic and multifarious and hence a source of creative energy. "The margin," wrote Robert Nunn, talking about post-colonialism and Canadian theatre, "is no longer the periphery but the frontier, the place of possibility."

We don't have to look so far afield for evidence of the struggle to find a discrete cultural identity after centuries of domination by England. The debate about a national theatre and the ambivalent position of a "home" colony that was complicit in British imperialism has also been debated in Scotland. Those arguments about achieving a cultural consciousness without the accompanying political, economic or legal independence, apply to Scotland as much as Wales, of course. But in several ways Scotland is a separate case. What has happened in the past fifteen years or so, and especially in Glasgow, is that theatre (indeed, the arts in general) has been reclaimed. The Scottish Trades Union Congress became involved in promoting the arts and their founding of the Mayfest had the brief to "celebrate not only May

18

Day but also Scottish working-class theatre and popular political theatre from other countries". The Scottish TUC has its own arts officer and has put the arts on the political agenda. When Glasgow was made City of Culture in 1990, the local council gave some £26 million pounds for projects involving indigenous artists (including the diverse "ethnic" cultures within the region). Intervention by Scotland's local authorities not only made the Scottish Arts Council's funding look miserly but, crucially, ensured that local needs and values were made important. If only local authorities and trade unions in Wales - traditionally the popular backbone of the nation - had invested in theatre as a crucial element in creating a cultural independence! Scotland's example makes the idea of a national theatre company redundant, because theatre (to an extent) is in the hands of and relates to local people - in fact the proposal for a central national theatre company was thrown out in 1995. Wales, as we shall see, has its culture controlled not by its democratically-elected representatives or its artists but by a power élite. And Wales is unlike Scotland in other ways, not least in the absence of any visible theatre tradition.

Research perhaps underestimates attendances when it claims getting on for half the population of Wales (41%) go to the theatre at least once a year - although this is far higher than England. For a small country of under three million (the same size as, say, Latvia) and only three major conurbations, that's a pretty high level of activity and support. But is it just my own bias as a theatre critic that makes me wonder why these achievements are so little celebrated? If my thesis is correct, then theatre is the medium through which is expressed the search for cultural identity, in which we might hear the authentic voice of the difference of this small country, far more than The National Eisteddfod. So why the low profile in Wales (small wonder it has a low profile over the border) when a lot of people go, and not just to theatres like the New. Theatr Iolo, for example, will stage five shows a year to around 15,000 people in 200 different venues - none of them theatre buildings. Unlike England, there is hardly any location in Wales that does not have theatre available to it. It is the most democratic of the arts as well as the most popular. But apart from Antony Hopkins is there a Welsh theatre practitioner known to most Welsh people? Are there any playwrights, directors, designers or actors in any decision-making political positions, as in other European and Latin-American countries? Do any make news? Are theatre practitioners, in brief, highly regarded members of Welsh society? No. Next to rugby players, they are nonentities. What sort of nationalism are we talking about that disregards any artist, especially those that are in the vanguard of redefining cultural identity? After all, Welshness was once defined solely in terms of its (nontheatrical) performance arts, poetry and music.

Why wasn't Y Cwmni's *House of America*, or Volcano's *L.O.V.E.*, or Brith Gof's *Pax*, for example, all award-winners outside Wales and seen all over Europe, celebrated as a source of national pride? A National Theatre of Wales, it's suggested, could redress the balance by raising the profile. Welsh theatre, as others have pointed out (notably playwright Ed Thomas), is all but invisible inside as well as outside Wales. Wales, indeed, is invisible.

So why is theatre in Wales seen as so irrelevant? Why can the media ignore theatre in the knowledge that in popular terms, it is unimportant - despite the quantity, quality and attendance?

I suspect that there is a kind of simplistic nationalism which actually militates against real explorations of nationality by tacitly supporting "national" stereotypes. In broad popular-culture terms, Wales is a nation of song, coal and rugby - still, despite all the evidence to the contrary! - and its only contribution to theatre has been superstar actors Richard Burton and Anthony Hopkins, boozer writer Dylan Thomas (whose radio play rarely works well on stage) and Emlyn Williams's *The Corn is Green*. In other words, Wales has taken on board the "orientalism" of its English colonisers: a Wales that was an English invention, just as the Orient is a Western invention.

Then, the cult of amateurism still holds sway, with professional arts regarded with suspicion. (I still witness community venue organisers thanking a highly professional company after a show for "giving up their time" to provide people with entertainment!) There is perhaps still the idea that real popular theatre is actually amateur theatre and that subsidised professional theatre is the embodiment of the imposed Anglicised establishment "high art" that did indeed make much popular culture invisible in Wales. Or is amateurism the validation of that colonial "inferiorism" that is hinted at in the national stereotyping and orientalisation I just referred to? And while performance has been part of Welsh culture for longer than most other European nations, the provision of professional theatre in Wales is actually less than thirty years old.

Psychologists tell us that the moment we become a human individual is when we first look in a mirror and know that we see ourselves. This happens at anything from six to eighteen months, later for autistic children, and only with humans and certain chimpanzees. It is an indication of consciousness. What do we see in that mirror? We see another that is also us - a moment that can be one of alienation or autonomy. Theatre conventionally is described as a society examining its reflection: "The purpose of playing," says Hamlet, is "to hold the mirror up to nature". If those psychologists are right then that mirror is not simply a reflection but a crucial stage in the search for identity. (The influential psychoanalyst Lacan uses the phrase "mirror stage" deliberately as a pun to suggest both a developmental moment and an arena of conflict for humanity.) Perhaps it has taken until now for the Welsh to imagine themselves, as regards their culture, not just reflectively but crucially in their relationship with the world - a real "cultural consciousness".

Finally, on the vexed subject of nationalism, we must come to the crunch, to move from theory to actuality, to face up to what some call "the R-word". We may examine the benefits of being a marginalized, perhaps post-colonial, culture; at the same time, though, there is inevitably a defensive, protective nationalistic response to colonization. It is where the positive effects of a search for cultural identity topples over into the familiar abyss of embracing the myth of nationalism. It is a myth based on invented traditions. It insists that a nation is not an "imagined community" or a "created community" but a homogenous monoglot society, rooted in tradition, language and culture. Those Welsh inhabitants whose predecessors arrived from Asia or Africa or even as close as Poland and Italy, and not as colonizers like the English, could never qualify as *Cymry* and would be excluded from "the nation". This is perhaps the most disturbing aspect to certain kinds of nationalism and arguably is implicit in the idea of a National Theatre.

When much of the theatre world, in America and Europe, is exploring with urgency the problems of multiculturalism and interculturalism, a lot of Welsh theatre seems far more concerned with its own cultural navel-gazing. And I do wonder just why, when issues about language and nationalism have been exhaustively tackled by Welsh theatre, issues about multiculturalism have not? When South Wales has one of the strongest National Front memberships in Britain, when fascist rock bands flourish, when far-right organizations collaborate with Welsh Nationalist groups, why has there been no recognition of all this on stage if theatre is really the art form most sensitive to the lived experience and its problems? According to the latest figures, racial attacks in Wales have increased by 325 per cent over the last five years. There were more racist incidents in the three Glamorgans than in any other of the UK's 43 police areas, outside London and Manchester. And yet to my knowledge there has not been, with the notable exception of the work of the now defunct Theatr Taliesin, a single theatre production that acknowledges Wales's cultural diversity or even Cardiff's multicultural mix - it is, after all, Britain's oldest-established multicultural society - on the main stage or even in community work. (Alan Osborne's *Tiger! Tiger!* for Moving Being was about the rise of industrial Cardiff but avoided racial politics, Tim Green's *Race*, for the now Gradual Decline company, was essentially historical, and Theatr Iolo devised a theatre-in-education project. Ironically, at least one play dealing with racism -based on a true event in Merthyr, by Dic Edwards - was rejected by the BBC for its Welsh Playhouse series, I understand, because of its subject-matter.)

Steve Fletcher, a co-founder of Theatr Taliesin and now development officer of South Wales Intercultural Community Arts, has campaigned for years and can still say how he finds it "sadly ironic" that many who passionately advance the concern for Welsh cultural identity seem unable to extend that basic right to self-expression to those ethnic minorities who have chosen to make Wales their home. He claims the single most significant piece of evidence in the case against what many see as a Welsh cultural ruling élite is the inability of the Arts Council of Wales (and its predecessor) to make any kind of meaningful statement (let alone policy or even realistic resource allocation) on multicultural arts in Wales. Indeed the official response, after much pressure, to questions of cultural diversity in a changing Wales remains a "multicultural" arts policy issued by the (then) Welsh Arts Council in 1989. It formally reaffirmed support for "indigenous" Welsh work, especially work in Welsh, and in a brief document that is startlingly ignorant and insensitive it suggests that "awareness of difference, and of the value of a multi-cultural situation, should create a more sympathetic approach in Wales to non-Welsh (sic) cultures...[which] is, ironically, jeopardised if support for non-Welsh cultures is perceived to be at the expense of Welsh-language culture". It notes the "deeply-felt aversion of many Welsh-speakers to any link with policies intended to deal with the multi-racial nature of British society...the Arts Council should not mix up its duty towards the Welsh language with its duty towards ethnic minority arts." This outrageously inept single-sheet policy drafted by Tom Owen, at the time director of the Welsh Arts Council, still stands as official policy. It is such institutionalized ideas of Wales and "multiculturalism" that makes me fear that a National Theatre, which would inevitably be absorbed by the artistic, ideological hegemony of the Taffia that controls institutional life in Wales,

23

would be likely (in spite of the anti-nationalist and multicultural principles of people like Michael Bogdanov and Phil Clark) to reinforce the inherent racism of the arts establishment.

Identity

Cultural domination of Wales by England has conventionally resulted in an "anglicization" that started in the Renaissance, accelerated in the Industrial Revolution and took hold when all Welsh children were taught English and so were introduced to the largest canon of literature in the world and all the ideological clout it carries. Handel and Byron, we have to remember, are Welsh Christian names from English cultural icons (and Haydn also came via the English).

Of course, exposure to English-language work was ideologically not solely imperialist or even capitalist. The Plebs League (founded in 1909) and the upsurge in working-class self-education, the miners' institute libraries and the Workers' Education Association from the 1930s to recently, all centred on a radical anti-bourgeois reading-list based on English, not Welsh, texts, often imported from America. The American Connection is strong: apart from the legends of Madoc and the Mandan "Welsh Indians", Welsh agitators had been supporters of the American Revolution (and, of course, the French Revolution that followed it) and five of the signatories of the American Declaration of Independence were Welsh; Welsh settlements were established in the USA and Canada, and later Patagonia, as emigrants looked to establish a new Wales outside Britain. Sir Alfred Zimmerman had spoken of an American Wales (along with a Welsh Wales and an English Wales) in the 1920s; Gwyn Thomas wrote of his childhood that "places like the Rhondda were parts of America that never managed to get on the boat". Ed Thomas's most articulate play on cultural identity is *House of America,* where his Welsh family are obsessed by Westerns, Jack Kerouac, The Doors and Hendrix. And it was the works of Jack

London, Upton Sinclair, Sinclair Lewis and other left-wing popular American authors that were read in the 1930s by a generation who had had to learn English and for whom the radical populism would strike chords. Americanization, it can be argued, could have positive sides as well.

But crucially it is not only When Was Wales? but Where Was Wales? Ed Thomas has with bitter humour repeatedly asked how a nation that has Harry Secombe as its idol can take itself seriously. Lest Harry Secombe take offence, I would extend the pantheon to Max Boyce, Tom Jones, Ruth Madoc and various other "professional Welsh". The image of the Welsh nation to outsiders is characterized, or rather caricaturized, by stereotypes: those stars and anonymous symbols like The Miner, The Eisteddfod Bard, The Minister, The Rugby Player and The Mam. And, alas, it is a portrait of national stereotypes that too many Welsh people and institutions assimilate.

The lack of self-esteem, as Ed Thomas was pointing out in *House of America* and in his plays' repeated jokes about the likes of Harry Secombe and Tom Jones, makes it difficult to talk about identity and, indeed, to discover one. I would cautiously suggest that it may be impossible to write an authentic Welsh play today simply because it is so difficult to create real characters who are Welsh, so institutionalized in the culture is the array of stereotypes. By the same token, a National Theatre of Wales may be a meaningful impossibility because it could not be authentic.

This is not as extreme as it may at first seem. If we look at the theories of discourse and power - that is, how power is expressed through culture as much as the more obvious forms of oppression - we can see, for example, how in the eighteenth and nineteenth centuries Britain and France (and more recently America) created an artificial "Orient" that was unrecognizable by people who lived there but was an essential part of the colonial exercise of power by the West over the East. China, Japan, India, all subjects of Western political ambition, were recreated by Western writers and artists in terms that reaffirmed the imperialists' superiority (as they saw it) - not conscious, deliberate colonialism but as necessary and as expressive of the perceived power relationship as armed forces and architecture.

A similar political discourse can be seen in Britain, where England (in the name of Britain, or less evocatively The United Kingdom) "colonized" Wales (and Ireland and Scotland, of course) as much as it had India and Africa. An artificial "Wales" was created through English literature and art, one that unwittingly echoed the very meaning of the name of the neighbour-colony by seeing it as "foreign". (This concurrently with encouraging the popular belief in Anglo-Celtic unification, imperial greatness and patriotism that created quite another sense of national identity, Britishness, that still exists: patriotism in Wales can be both Welsh nationalism and British jingoism.)

Writer-travellers like Gray, Gilpin, and Wordsworth, who saw the landscape rather as geographic correlatives to mental states, and artists like Sandby, Turner, Girtin, Rowlandson, Cotman, Cox and the Varleys, between 1750 and 1850 celebrated Picturesque Wales with an enthusiasm that confirmed the Englishman's view of the land as rugged, unspoilt and peopled by rustic characters - so unlike rational, organized, powerful England - and created Wales as a tourist attraction. The coded politics of the "Picturesque" was, of course, more than imperialism: it is also sexual, an example of the powerful, possessive "male gaze" that creates a female of the landscape - something that contributed to the later Victorian idea of "wild Welsh women". Poet Thomas Gray's *The Bard* not only romanticized the land but helped create the hoary-haired bearded bard image - and Gray hadn't even been on a day trip to Conway's foaming flood when he wrote the poem in 1757 (unlike most of the dozen artists who interpreted the poem in the following sixty years). A hundred years later, George Borrow's *Wild Wales*, probably the most famous book written about Wales and ostensibly intended as a huge compliment (and indeed in content and intent one of the least patronizing of guides), can be seen as part of a literature that extolled a mythological country of ancient heroes and bards. This "orientalizing" of Wales fortuitously coincided with the romantic age so that such fanciful re-creation could be seen as a product of a genre rather than an expression of male, colonial power. But by a process of selective description, Wales was culturally defined in the way that it was useful for England to see it. (Ireland, significantly, defied such extensive cultural appropriation and the turning point, for both the culture and independence, came when Yeats and others "reclaimed" culture through the Gaelic League and thence the Irish Literary Theatre...and on to the Abbey Theatre, Easter Rising and Irish Free State.)

So English travel-writers, historians and critics perpetuated the "otherness" of the land beyond Offa's Dyke, attributing all sorts of characteristics to the Welsh. Matthew Arnold praised their style and magic as "Celts" but would, I suspect, have condemned the real people as celebrating "anarchy" rather than "culture" in his famous division of society; while the English praised the independence, spirit and imagination of those strange neighbours, men like Arnold seem not to have noticed that in his own lifetime the quaint Celts had made bloody rebellion in the Merthyr Rising, the Chartist Riots and the Rebecca Riots. Even Gladstone, who (as the squire of Hawarden with a Welsh wife) ostensibly supported Welsh culture and language, spoke about the nation in terms of ancient tradition and history; as he addressed eisteddfod audiences, Welsh was not even taught in schools and Wales was fast becoming an economically depressed area with severe rural depopulation, urban poverty and widespread ill-health, just like what we might today term a third-world colony.

It was an "Other" that the English colonists romantically orientalized, racially denigrated or imperiously ignored. While the 1819 Peterloo Massacre, where several protesters were shot during a demonstration in Manchester, caused shock waves and banner headlines throughout England, the shooting of twenty-four Welsh protesters twenty or so years later during the Merthyr Rising was virtually ignored by the London press. During the Rebecca Riots of the "hungry forties" London and

Liverpool theatres staged a production called *Rebecca and Her Daughters* that never reached Wales: hardly surprising, since it was a musical farce with a synopsis that went like this: "Mysterious appearance of Rebecca and her daughters in the glen at Llandeilo at midnight - Trial before the justice of [the] peace - Happy denouement". Plays that did reach Wales reinforced the romantic mythology while, perhaps, cannily exploiting renewed nationalistic interest: *Llewellyn, Last of the Princes*, *The Last of the Welsh Bards* and *The Maid of Cefn Ydfa* were all toured round Wales by English-based portable theatres in the 1870s.

To the English imperialists, the Welsh were a people who, like all natives, were in need of instruction, conversion and control. The notorious "Blue Books", the 1847 *Report on the State of Education in Wales*, not only described the Welsh language as a barrier to moral progress and facilitating perjury in the courts but officially established the Welsh as degenerate: they were dirty, ignorant, bigoted and contented; promiscuous; wanting chastity; immoral; violent and vicious; and so on, according to various witnesses. The London press had a field day, with the *Morning Chronicle* wallowing in racism and calling for the Welsh language to be banned, claiming that "Wales is fast settling down into the most savage barbarity".

It is a portrait that historian Jane Aaron has charted in her work on the depiction of Welsh women in Victorian and Edwardian fiction: "Hoydens of Wild Wales", they were uncontrolled, sexual, irresponsible. The notion of the "exotic" (and that is how the Welsh were by now seen) female as being sexually available, especially to the colonizing Englishman, or at best in need of correction by the superior English male, is a theme that still runs through erotica. It was also paralleled, as I have said, by the implicit sexuality of landscape fetishism where Wales's picturesque contours are ripe for rape by the conquering coloniser (a sexual image echoed in Alexander Cordell's *Rape of the Fair Country*). Aaron's research has been into the depiction of these wild women not by Englishmen but by women novelists from Mrs Gaskill (in her novel *Ruth*, for example) to the less known Anne Beale, an English woman who settled in Llandeilo, and Allen Raine, a Welsh woman who had a home near New Quay but lived in England, whose heroines seem to be wanton simply because they live in Wild Wales.

The Welsh as constructed by the English colonial imagination were a mix of noble savages, ancient druidic bards and devious, promiscuous subversives. Of Shakespeare's Welsh characters, probably created specifically for a Welsh member of the theatre company, Owen Glendower is ridiculed by Hotspur as a tedious, wordy charlatan with his talk of magical powers, although Mortimer qualifies the portrait by calling him worthy, well-read, valiant, affable and bountiful as mines in India (an interesting colonial allusion) - the Welsh Henry Tudor was, after all, to found a dynasty that ended with Shakespeare's royal patron, Elizabeth. And it was in Tudor and Elizabethan London that the Welsh were probably most respected. Thereafter the fictional Welsh, on the rare occasions they featured in English literature, started to be parodies, stereotypes, "orientalized" natives, as in the novels of George Meredith (despite his half-Welsh parentage), and more recently John Cowper Powys (despite his name) and to some extent, and in a different way, A. J. Cronin and Alexander Cordell. By the time Kingsley Amis offered his versions in *That Uncertain Feeling*, filmed as *Only Two Can Play*, and *The Old Devils*, which revisits the "Aberdarcy" - Swansea - of the earlier novel, the archetypal Welshman was fixed in the culture.

Of course, not all the political discourse was coded. There was the simple racial stereotyping, from the children's nursery rhyme 'Taffy was a Welshman, Taffy was a thief,' first recorded around 1760, to the aforementioned Kingsley Amis. Hardly likely to instil self-esteem was the torrent of abuse in Edwardian times dressed up as satire, legitimized to an extent by Wales's own self-criticism: when Caradoc Evans's play *Taffy* played in London the theatre was almost destroyed by the angry audience, and while Arthur Tyssilio Johnson thought he was satirizing the anti-Welsh feelings of the Edwardian Home Rule period in his pseudonymous tract *The Perfidious Welshman*, actually there was little difference between the parody and the original. "His Majesty King Edward VII will endure anything for the sake of his people. He will listen to niggers' tom-toms and suffer a Cymric choir to bellow and shriek at him," wrote Johnson, or Draig Glas as he called himself. "Not only have we the Welshman's dialect, which is obviously a blend of Semitic and other tongues, but the cast of features, inferior intellect, excitability, deceitfulness and absurd vanity all seem to prove that Taffy is, for the most part, a remnant of the Mongolian race." Two years later, in 1912, the English satirist T.W.H. Crosland wrote in the so-say humorous *Taffy was a Welshman*: "The fact is that Wales is a little land, and the Welsh are a little people, with little intellects and little views." .... and worse. (The tradition of dubious self-criticism lives on: witness the recent *Xenophobe's Guide to The Welsh* - "cunning, loquacious, and motivated by a love of vendetta and other people's property"!) Another Englishman not known for his subtle satire, John Maynard Keynes, the great liberal economist and first head of the Arts Council, in 1919 described Lloyd George as "a goat-footed bard, a half-human visitor to our age from the hag-ridden magic and enchanted woods of Celtic antiquity" - in jest, of course. (In fact Keynes despised Lloyd George, whom he dubbed The Artful Dodger, for a lack of principle he attributed to the Prime Minister's "existence outside or away from our Saxon good and evil".)

The caricatured stereotype, physical and moral, was by now part of the English view of the Welsh. Who are these, described ten years later? "Ten men of revolting appearance...low of brow, crafty of eye, and crooked of limb. They advanced huddled together with the loping tread of wolves, peering about them furtively as they came, as though in constant terror of ambush; they slavered at their mouths, which hung loosely over their receding chins, while each clutched under his ape-like arm a burden of curious and unaccountable shape." Yes, it's a Welsh brass band, described by the same respected English wit who explained that the Welsh were not Celts but Iberians: "From the earliest times the Welsh have been looked upon as an unclean people. It is thus they have preserved their racial integrity. Their sons and daughters rarely mate with human-kind except their own blood relations...The Welsh are the only nation in the world that has produced no graphic or plastic art, no architecture, no drama. They just sing..sing and blow down wind instruments of plated silver. They are deceitful because they cannot discern truth from falsehood, depraved because they cannot discern the consequences of their indulgence." This was Evelyn Waugh in his 1928 best-selling novel *Decline and Fall*. Bernard Manning, eat your heart out.

It would be silly (and offensive) to suggest that England's attitude to Wales and the Welsh was on a par with other examples of western colonialists' exercise of power. The Welsh were not exhibited in the taverns, fairs, zoos, museums and theatres of London as were, say, the Cadigal people of South Sydney, Australia, or Saartje Benjamin, "The Hottentot Venus", or the "Laplander Family" (displayed with reindeer) or "Red Indians" or Bushmen or Kaffirs or "Pygmies" or the two microcephalic San Salvadorans billed as "the last Aztec survivors of a mysterious jungle city called Ixinaya", all of whom were on display as evidence of England's natural superiority between 1780 and 1880. But since Wales and the Welsh were neighbours of the English, that fascination with "otherness" could be conveniently explored. The difference between the process of cultural colonization in India and Africa, say, and in Wales is geographical: hence my question Where Was Wales? Wales was a neighbour (with no visible border and its inhabitants, while apparently un-English in many ways, white) and instead of just being part of the Empire was also part of a smaller and cosier unit, the Kingdom. And the native language had been suppressed far more than in the further reaches of Empire, with every Welsh child learning English at school (and later, of course, being punished for not speaking English with the notorious Welsh Not around the neck). How much more inevitable, then, that the Wales manufactured by the English, the foreignness was that created by the colonists as part of their exercise of ideological power rather than one of real cultural difference, was accepted by the "foreigners" themselves. By the time of the calls for Home Rule in the 1880s Wales was defined in terms of Wild Wales, the Eisteddfod, The Picturesque, Lloyd Georgian rhetoric, The Celtic Fringe - terms dictated by English imperialists but actually to a large extent accepted by the Welsh. And not just accepted, but celebrated. Without wishing to over-generalize, much Welsh writing (especially, apparently, Welsh-language literature) after the First World War, when Wales was struggling to find a cultural identity in that earlier period of ideological doubt, owed much to the pastoral idyll. Wales was "a Garden of Eden entered by courtesy of the Great Western Railway", as Kenneth O. Morgan put it. Those clichés, and the way that the exploited industrial workers in iron, steel and coal were safely converted into noble savages by the same hegemony, are ones that still define national identity as represented in cultural products from *Under Milk Wood* to The Big Pit Museum by way of comedians and male voice choirs. And it continues: the *Welsh Arts Season 1995* brochure, promoted by the Wales Tourist Board, opens "Wales. A land of legend and enchantment, of ancient kings and wizards, of craggy mountain peaks, lush valleys and unspoilt coastlines, where fairytale castles tower against the skies and tiny villages nestle in the hills..." So much for art.

No wonder cultural confusion reigns. On one hand, contemporary Wales can be seen as an ideological construct, a product of political discourse, an "Other" invented by a neighbouring oppressor, translated into and assumed as a set of stereotypes, often expressed in purely racist terms; on the other, absorbed by England and America into an amorphous anonymity with no individual identity, invisible even, echoing still that notorious 1910 *Encyclopaedia Brittanica* entry "For Wales, see England".

Of course not the only cultural product to come out of Wales today (or indeed historically) is one that reinforces or accepts the English "orientalization" of Wales or the more obvious

Anglicisation and Americanisation - especially in the Welsh language, many writers have always attempted to speak with an authentic Welsh voice. But it is increasingly difficult to dismantle the "orientalizing" images and to deny the effects of Anglo-American mass popular culture and I would suggest that most works today that seek to mediate an authentic national identity are not expressions of popular culture but of either the (linguistically) ethnic minority or academia.

It isn't that simple, anyway. I am not talking just about conventional cultural influences, but about what I call (after Edward Said) Wales's "orientalization" and subsequent self-acceptance of the power relationships implicit in that political discourse. How possible is it to find a Welsh voice as we enter the twenty-first century and the whole idea of indigenous cultural consciousness is questionable? Just as class consciousness may have been made redundant by the imposition of a false consciousness created and imposed by late capitalism, so cultural consciousness may be an impossibility in the face of the same ideology. It may be that "Welshness" is so much a product of English oppression that it can have no true meaning. It is a contention that we will find when we look later at theatre companies which are all about articulating national identity. But I do fear that a National Theatre of Wales, albeit espoused by sincere Welsh people, could be yet another English-inspired invention.

ENTR'ACTE

Democracy is skin-deep in Wales. Because the people persist recently in voting against Conservatism in both parliamentary and local government elections, the rulers have to exercise control by by-passing democracy. The Government, through the Welsh Office, controls over one hundred bodies where appointments are made by the Secretary of State and the country is virtually run by quangos - quasi-autonomous non-governmental organizations or, in other words, committees with apparent independence but actually set up by the government and made up entirely of government appointees. There are over fifty such quangos in Wales, from the Welsh Development Agency, Wales Tourist Board and Arts Council of Wales to smaller, but often quite vital organizations, and between them they are responsible for a staggering 80% of public expenditure. (This figure, like all the data here, is correct at the time of writing; details and names may have changed by the time you read this, but the principles, I suspect, won't have.) There are those, of course, who would suggest that Wales has always been run by quangos and together they are known as the "Great and the Good", and not necessarily obvious Conservatives either. You might include The Taffia or Freemasons or The Old School Tie within this or see them as a separate influence; certainly one report into Welsh quangos suggested that the main qualification for serving was "a funny handshake".

Relatively few people (in the quangos, 250 part-time salaried nominees of the Secretary of State for Wales) are part of this power elite and their motives are mixed. Basically, of course, they share an ideology about how society should be organized and they can exercise this through a variety of cultural institutions - from apparently non-political networks based on the Friends of the Welsh National Opera, Masonic Lodges, National Eisteddfod, Cardiff and County Club, and so on, to the quangos and trusts and local authorities. Wales is a small country, run to all intents and purposes from Cardiff, a small city, and the hegemony is easily maintained.

Who controls the arts in Wales? Not who you'd think. There are the obvious main funders: the Arts Council of Wales, the Lottery and, to a diminishing extent, the local authorities. The most important body is or should be the Arts Council - a quango whose fifteen members are all appointed by the Secretary of State for Wales. The Lottery is administered by the Arts Council with its own unelected lottery board. The local authorities contribute to the arts with grants to organizations, with the aim of "parity" funding between the Arts Council and local authority. Bodies such as Cardiff Bay Development Corporation, Welsh Development Agency, Development Board for Rural Wales, Wales Tourist Board and Cadw, for example, sponsor art activities. The BBC and S4C are major patrons of the arts. The universities and colleges obviously play a major role, too. There are also trusts like Cardiff Bay Arts Trust, Cardiff Bay Opera House Trust - and, now (or so it seems at the time of writing), a National Theatre of Wales Trust.

The exercise of patronage, you might think, is therefore wide. Not so. Firstly, one unnamed body is behind all these organizations: the Welsh Office. Then to an extent a handful or so of influential individuals decide what happens - because they hold the purse-strings. Call them The Great and the Good or The Taffia, they are of similar backgrounds with similar business interests and with similar personal and political agendas. Some of the names and positions that follow may, like some other statistics, have changed between the writing and publication of this essay; but I suspect not much else.

Is this paranoia, conspiracy theory gone mad? No, it is *realpolitik*. For example, look briefly at the biggest of Wales's quangos, the Welsh Development Agency: a Commons Public Accounts Committee savaged the organization in 1993 so much that the whiz-kid brought in to run it, Dr Gwyn Jones, resigned - but Dr Jones is still on other quangos. Though he has left the Welsh Water Enterprise Board, the Prince of Wales Committee,

The Prince's Youth Business Trust and BT Wales Advisory Board, Dr Jones as I write is (according to *Who's Who*) still instrumental in Wales's cultural life as the BBC National Governor for Wales and an appointee to the board of S4C, not to mention his responsibilities on the Council of the University of Wales and the Court of University College, Swansea, and his membership of the board of the Welsh National Opera. How fortunate he was to bump into the then Welsh Secretary, Peter Walker, at a dinner party and so persuade the minister that he was destined to be more than Conservative Party prospective parliamentary candidate for Clwyd North West .

Or take another quango-run enterprise, Cardiff Bay: a scheme which in its entirety, especially the barrage, was opposed by most people. Responsible organizations concerned with the environment invoked European law. According to every principle of democracy the scheme should have been abandoned or modified. It got through. Because a few powerful people wanted it, needed it, to go through. If those same people back the National Theatre of Wales, that too will become a reality; and while no-one makes money out of the arts in any obvious way, we should perhaps wonder why Wales's power elite would back the idea.

Cardiff Bay Development Corporation does contribute much to the arts, of course, from Bay Days to concerts, and was the conduit for Welsh Office funding for the Cardiff Opera House Trust. Doubtless CBDC chairman Geoffrey Inkin (another former Tory candidate and also Chairman of the Land Authority for Wales, another quango) discusses cultural issues with fellow directors Hugh Hudson Davies, Alan Cox of ASW and Cardiff Tory leader Jeff Sainsbury in the Cardiff and County Club, where they (along with many of the great and good men) are members (entrance fee currently £810, annual membership £410, membership by invitation only). Ex-CBDC board member Ann Robinson (a former Tory Euro-candidate and currently head of the Institute of Directors' Policy Unit) wouldn't be allowed in the Cardiff and County, or the Freemasons, but she was able to

36

exchange opinions with fellow CBDC directors Hugh Hudson Davies, Geoffrey Inkin and Donald Walters at Welsh National Opera board meetings, where they are all directors, or (until recently) Arts Council of Wales meetings, where Hugh Hudson Davies was also a member, along with (until 1994) Mathew Prichard, whose fortune is based on Agatha Christie royalties and who is, inevitably, another Cardiff and County Club member.

Mathew Prichard, who was also Chairman of Cardiff Bay Arts Trust, Vice-President of the Council of the National Museum of Wales and Chairman of the Opera House Trust, was appointed Chairman of the Arts Council by his cousin, Lord Crickhowell, then simply Welsh Secretary Nicholas Edwards. Lord Crickhowell, we were grateful to see, after leaving office continued his public involvement in the arts as Chairman of Cardiff Bay Opera Trust, a director of HTV, President of University College Cardiff, President of the Contemporary Arts Society of Wales and former director of the board of the Welsh National Opera (where Lady Crickhowell fortunately then kept the family interest alive); and he does manage to fit it all in between his other quango appointment with the National Rivers Authority and board meetings of Anglesey Mining and Associated British Ports Holdings (who own much of Cardiff Bay). At least he also can relax in the Cardiff and County with his mates.

Ann Robinson, by the way, isn't the only woman to be invited into the male-dominated world of arts patronage. Sherilyn Bankes, who with her stockbroker husband met the then Welsh Secretary David Hunt at a Conservative function in Mold, suddenly found herself elevated from editor of the Friends of Theatr Clwyd newsletter to being invited to sit as a full member of the Arts Council. How unlike another colleague, Jane Davidson, for years a member of the Arts Council's advisory Drama Committee whose membership of the decision-making full Council was blocked by Ian Grist, then MP for Cardiff Central and Welsh Under-Secretary, until she dropped her aspirations to become a Labour MP for his constituency.

Other power brokers in the arts include, or included until

recently, Sir Donald Walters, former Chairman of the Welsh Conservative Party, Chairman of the Council of University College of Wales Cardiff, Deputy Chairman of the WDA and a board member of the Development Board for Rural Wales and the Welsh National Opera; Sir Idris Pearce, yet another former Tory candidate and property tycoon, is Chair of the Higher Education Funding Council (on which the active Ms Robinson also sits); Geraint Stanley Jones, former S4C boss and still a powerful voice, is on the Arts Council of Wales, the Lottery Board and the WNO board and is yet another Cardiff and County Club man; David Bowen Lewis, a millionaire, was Vice-Chairman of the Arts Council of Wales and former Director of the Wales Crafts Council; Lord Crickhowell, Mathew Prichard, Ann Robinson, Alan Cox and Hugh Hudson Davies I have already mentioned. The man who might seem to be overlord of arts funding, the executive Director of the Arts Council of Wales, Emyr Jenkins, seems positively modest: former IBA Wales Advisory Committee and Welsh Language Education Development Committee member, honorary member of the Gorsedd of Bards and Elder of the Presbyterian Church of Wales. The new Arts Council of Wales, actually, is far less top-heavy with the power-élite, although the new chairman, Sir Richard Jones KCB, was Under-Secretary at the Welsh Office. But it should be clear by now that real power and authority resides in the hands of people who operate in the world of business, banking, law and property. They meet at the Cardiff and County Club and at their masonic lodges, where they mix with politicians, accountants, judges, financiers, industrialists, developers and policemen.

I would never suggest any impropriety or corruption in the Welsh arts world, of course, merely the concentration of decision-making power in so few hands. But is it not interesting that on the Arts Council of Wales (annual arts budget £15million) were until recently Mathew Prichard, David Bowen Lewis, Hugh Hudson Davies, Ann Robinson, David L. Williams and Geraint Stanley Jones; on the Lottery board (distributing an estimated

£15million) are Hugh Hudson Davies and Geraint Stanley Jones; on Cardiff Bay Opera House Trust, Lord Crickhowell, Lord Davies of Llandinam, Mathew Prichard, Sir John Tooley and David L. Williams; on the board of the Welsh National Opera (receiving £2million from ACW), who would have been tenants of the proposed opera house, are the names of Crickhowell, Lord Davies, Hudson Davies, Inkin, Jones, Stanley Jones, Robinson, Tooley, Walters and Williams; and on the board of Cardiff Bay Development Corporation, who channelled some £2million of Welsh Office funds (that is, public money) to the Cardiff Bay Opera House Trust (to no avail as it happened), Inkin, Hudson Davies, Robinson, Cox and Sainsbury. (For comparison I should point out that, for example, in 1994-5 Wales's leading theatre companies, Volcano Theatre and Y Cwmni, received around £50,000 each from ACW). The proposed Cardiff Bay Opera House was costed at £86.82 million but lest one think that there is any money motive, I must stress that tenders to build it (worth £46.5 million) would be dealt with through strict EC procurement procedures; and that Lord Crickhowell stood down as a member of the Opera House Trust during the sale to them of the land by Associated British Ports, of which he is a director.

So what individuals are we talking about when we come to the National Theatre of Wales? The prime movers, I am sure, are honourable men and I for one would never doubt their honesty, but their backgrounds indicate a common membership of a privileged cultural aristocracy. Michael Bogdanov was educated at Harrow, Trinity College, Dublin, The Sorbonne and Munich; Julian Mitchell at Winchester and Wadham College, Oxford; both are active supporters of and artists in the élitist world of opera (where they mix with Welsh political string-pullers Lord Crickhowell, Sir Donald Walters, Hugh Hudson Davies, Sir Geoffrey Inkin, Dr Gwyn Jones, Dr Ann Robinson, Sir Donald Walters and other WNO bigwigs). They may have different views about how a National Theatre could work, but they both subscribe to the principle; as educated, articulate, passionate, respected artists at the top of their profession, they move in high circles and have the ears of the highest in the land. They are both very likeable people, full of integrity and committed to theatre. Neither is a member of the Cardiff and County Club and neither to my knowledge is a Freemason. But despite being class mavericks they are inevitably, even unwittingly, part of the power élite.

II

Tradition

The search for authenticity can be a deceptive pastime but in Wales it seems particularly fruitless and disappointing. What, after all, are the symbols of real Welshness? The daffodil was allegedly adopted (by Lloyd George) when a printer accidentally substituted the flower for the leek in a 1907 publication. 'Hen Wlad Fy Nhadau' became the national anthem also as recently as around a hundred years ago after being composed as a Welsh air for the National Eisteddfod competition in 1858 by a publican and his son. And what about the National Eisteddfod? Invented, or at least in all the ritual, by a Glamorgan stonemason at the beginning of the last century. So-called "traditional" Welsh songs appeared at the same time. Male voice choirs came even later. The Welsh harp does not exist: it is Italian. Lovespoons? Not specifically Welsh, as you'd find if you went to Switzerland or Scandinavia. The national dress was invented by Lady Llanover in the 1860s, basing it on the tall black hats and tweed coats worn in remote areas in the 1790s after an English fashion of the 1620s. Rugby was introduced by English public-school-educated professional men and the first stars of the Welsh team were Englishmen like Hancock, Hellings, Packer, Watts, Boucher and Graham. And, worst of all, Max Boyce told me that most of his "Welsh" jokes were adaptations of stories he'd heard elsewhere - and *Oggi Oggi Oggi* is lifted from the Cornish.

We can no longer trust in tradition (it's fake) or history (it's nostalgia) or our idea of the "real" (there are no certainties today).

Is there such a thing as Welsh theatre? All theatre produced in Wales is, by simple definition, Welsh, of course. The context of every production is specific to the time and place, Wales today, with its economics, social structures, politics, cultural environment, landscape - and, yes, traditions. Naturally theatre in Wales is distinctive and distinctively Welsh.

However, conventional wisdom (and official policy) is that there was no theatre in Wales until it was imposed by the Arts Council in 1962 with the invention of the Welsh Theatre Company. I don't believe it. It is true that strictly speaking a documented history of theatre in Wales does not exist, and quite why drama is apparently absent from the long-established culture of Wales would make a subject for an intriguing book. And while other nations examined themselves through the medium of theatre, the Welsh did not - even allowing for the possibility that it was not so much a lack but a presence that was not recognized, noticed and recorded.

Perhaps people have been looking for the wrong animal - an English-style literary theatre. After all, ritual, pagan and religious, in which lie the origins of drama, must have played a part in prehistoric and Celtic tribal life in west Britain as much as in all civilizations. What do the history books tell us? That Wales, in the Caerleon amphitheatre, has one of the oldest performance spaces in Europe - but Roman, not Celtic. Of the Dark Ages stirrings of theatrical activity that led in other parts of Europe to liturgical plays, morality plays, miracle and mystery plays and Renaissance drama there is little evidence in Wales. We have some religious and secular medieval plays in Welsh, including equivalents of the miracle plays, probably written in north-east Wales during the second half of the fifteenth century, but no record of them having been staged: they are the kind that were part of the popular cycles performed by the craftspeople in English cities, and with no equivalent guild system or large cities in Wales performances must have been limited and certainly not part of any tradition or development. Travelling Welsh theatre companies performed in England (notably Shrewsbury) in the sixteenth century - but in English. A poetic drama (or dramatic poem, rather) of around 1600 based on Troilus and Cressida is the first full-length play in Welsh recorded and was probably never, and not meant to be, performed. The first acknowledged Welsh playwright, Twm o'r Nant (Thomas Edwards, the omission of whose name in either form from standard theatre reference books suggests that he and his fellows were little known outside Wales although George "Wild Wales" Borrow translated his work), brought a kind of popular theatre to the people in the late eighteenth century in a form that had been abandoned in England over a century before, the Interlude - an English term that no more describes the Welsh *anterliwt* as it does the French *intremet*, the Italian *tramesso*, *intermedio* and *intermezzo*, or the Spanish *entreme*. Twm was self-educated, a farm labourer, whose rural working-class background clearly adds to his literary reputation. His band of players delighted fair-goers and offended the English and, though described as amateurs, they did get paid - charging a penny per person they could earn 30 shillings (in other words, audiences of 350 or so) a night. Twm o'r Nant, born in 1738, died 1810, was a contemporary of Sheridan and Colman but is a long way from English and Anglo-Irish sophistication - indeed, he would jeer at the gentry, parsons and doctors who queued up to see the English comedies offered by touring companies. His importance in Wales at the time should not be underestimated: not only has his name passed into literary history but the number of portraits of him (four were painted in just one year) suggests that he was seen at the time as a major figure.

But it is in the *anterliwt,* popular in Wales for several hundred years, that we have a clue to the existence of a kind of indigenous Welsh theatre: it is, perhaps, the link between pre-medieval folk performance and later, more recognizable, drama. Crucially, in its eighteenth-century form it fitted into the indigenous bardic and moralising tradition and writers like Twm o'r Nant, Elis Roberts and half-a-dozen or so others created the only recorded Welsh contribution to theatre history. Before the early *anterliwtiau*, we can look for the origins of an indigenous tradition in the early bardic oral poetry that was created to be performed, not simply read or spoken, and may have developed from Celtic shamanism. The sixth-century declamatory verse of Taliesin and Aneirin was similarly as much performance as poetry. Put alongside this the continuous existence of possible developments of processional and religious rites, from mummings to *nosweithiau llawen* and the *Mari Lwyd* and other "folk" custom, we might construct a development of professional and community performance that bears little resemblance to other European drama but which would still qualify as Welsh theatre. What is important, though, is that while we must adjust our view that there was no theatre in Wales before this century the sort of performance we can claim as a theatre tradition is, nevertheless, all but invisible and left no legacy for us today.

What Welsh theatre lacked at crucial stages was, of course, patronage. Though early Welsh courts did employ the bard as a paid performer, *diddanwr*, and we have the patronized poetry actually classified as by *Beirdd yr Uchelwyr* (Poets of the Nobility), this had died out just at the time when England's kings and aristocracy started establishing what was to become English theatre. The English dramatic route was from tournaments to pageants and miracle plays to masques and morality plays to interludes to Shakespeare and his contemporaries; in Wales drama, it seems, remained a popular, often participatory, activity that like the rest of the culture was changed by Methodism. The church both opposed theatre and absorbed it - Twm o'r Nant's often ribald *anterliwtiau* ironically survived in preaching styles and in the *ymddiddanion*, moralistic dramatic monologues delivered in chapels, harking back to medieval morality theatre.

But then, crucially, or perhaps ironically, in conflict with Nonconformist condemnation, it was the revival of the eisteddfodau which led to more written drama and amateur performances - not the discovery of an indigenous theatre form or the invention of a new one, but the parodying of an artistically and socially bankrupt literary "domestic realism".

Invention

The first National Theatre movement, then, was based on a fake. The drama it espoused was not part of any indigenous performance tradition but a copy of the English (and recent Irish) literary theatre in its naturalist or realist phase, and also wedded to the alien building-based tradition. But it was bolstered by incipient nationalism.

It was Lloyd George's championing of Welsh drama at the Bangor National Eisteddfod in 1902 that sowed the seeds of the National Theatre movement that was to flourish sporadically from Lord Howard de Walden's patronage just before and after the First World War. Nationalism also shadowed the second attempt at a National Theatre in the 1930s, after the founding of Plaid Cymru and with the dynamism of Saunders Lewis. And again renewed nationalist activity provided the context for the third attempt in the 1960s, nationalism which led to the election of Gwynfor Evans as the first Plaid MP and which saw the re-emergence of Saunders Lewis to boost Welsh-language militancy and the new calls for a National Theatre - but by now the politics were even more confused. In 1959 the St David's Trust had been formed to campaign for a national company and a building; by 1961 there was an artist's impression in the press; in 1963 a brochure gave specific details; then, bizarrely, the St David's Trust announced that their 1500-seater building was to be opened in Investiture Year, 1969 - by the newly-created Prince of Wales! The current revival, The Welsh National Theatre Movement Phase 4, is, unlike earlier campaigns, not part of a resurgence in nationalist interest but no more, it seems to me, than the product of the coincident interests of a few well-intentioned individuals. Although, we could be forgiven for thinking that the earlier campaigns were no less concerned with individual interests.

Nevertheless, that cultural self-awareness (as distinct from nationalist sentiment) which had been lacking and which was essential for the creation of cultural product independent of the neighbouring power seems to have really developed only in the past twenty or thirty years. I leave it to historians and politicians to explain why, but the reason presumably has something to do in part with changing perceptions of nationalism, in part with the defusing of the language debate and in part with the example of other small nations claiming independence from their erstwhile oppressive neighbours. As I have suggested it has its parallel, perhaps, in post-colonial cultural expression all over the world - what Salman Rushdie means when he says "The Empire writes back to the centre". This suggests that the very "marginality" of colonised countries became a source of creative energy. The problem for Wales is that shared by other less-obviously colonised cultures - that while there is a creative energy in marginality, there can also be an attitude of being on the periphery, of looking towards the imperial centre which still controls policy, finance, exposure and status, that hinders the development of cultural autonomy and encourages the desertion of marginality. It is in Wales's rejection of the conventional English model of theatre that it is starting to succeed in expressing a sense of distinctive difference.

"Theatre" had to be invented, just as cultural identity had to be. The starting point back in the 1960s, when the Arts Council became the first real patron of theatre in Wales, was provision - establishing a theatre practice that delivered a product to as many people as possible. The first companies were, unlike others in Britain, deliberately created to tour to communities and schools rather than being an expression of practitioners' ambitions - although many of these rejected English models and were (and are) at the forefront of experimentation with style and form. Once the foundation of planned provision had been laid, things started to happen in the 1970s and theatre companies like no other evolved - Paupers Carnival, Cardiff Lab, Hijinx, Brith Gof, Magdalena, for example - which owed little to tradition. Indeed, even many so-say "planned provision" community/TIE companies rejected the English models and experimented with form. They came into being precisely because there was no tradition. With no major mainstream company outside Theatr Clwyd, there was no requirement to provide naturalistic drama either in terms of performance or playwriting. Style, form and content were based not on expectations (there were none, save those created by the community companies and they were all essentially non-naturalistic) but on the need to create new theatre in what was clearly and quickly becoming a new country with a new consciousness. The European work of innovators like Grotowski was an influence, but what was forged was something new.

Many practitioners, at least among the non-Welsh language speakers, are sceptical about the notion of Welshness applied to the theatre. At least, what they would say is that of course they are about Wales, because they live and work there. Playwrights in particular will point out that their work is a metaphor for the reality they are living: Dic Edwards, a Cardiff-born non-Welsh speaking writer now living in West Wales, set recent plays like *Utah Blue* and *The Man Who Gave His Foot for Love* in America and a Third World dictatorship, but beneath the plot they were about Wales; Charles Way's "western" *Dead Man's Hat*, underneath the genre label, is about Wales. Yet these and others would deny any concern with Welshness or cultural identity. But I think it is worth discussing, especially with the proposal for a National Theatre of Wales, whether there is now evolving, as I believe, something that we can identity as *Welsh theatre*, just as there is something we recognize as Polish theatre or French theatre. Whether it is in the Welsh or English language does not matter. The Magdalena Project or Cardiff Lab or Moving Being could have started anywhere: they in fact took root in Wales and because these innovatory, inspirational companies were there they helped create a theatre practice, a theatre ecology, that was distinctly different. A theatre genealogy was started which, with companies encouraged by the "otherness" of the theatrical "cultural climate", has developed into this identifiable Welsh theatre. A National Theatre does not feature in this theatre genealogy.

Diversity

What is the difference, then, if, as I have suggested, an "authentic" naturalistic conventional theatre in Wales is impossible? The critical effect of colonialism was stereotyping, imposed as part of the exercise of power by the colonizers and accepted as a result of cultural conditioning by the colonized: a generalization, of course, but it meant that theatre could not deal in characters and situations as could English or Scottish theatre. The only form of theatre that could address questions of Welshness (and arguably if every discourse is political and cultural then every piece of theatre produced in Wales does at some level contain an attitude, overt or coded, to identity) was, then, non- or anti-naturalism. Brith Gof realised this - "The forms, techniques, preoccupations and placement of a Welsh theatre may bear no relation to those of its English neighbour," Brith Gof's co-founder, Englishman Mike Pearson, told an international conference in 1985.

So what do we have in Wales today? Let us take a cross-section of theatre in Wales, half-a-dozen very different companies: say Brith Gof, Hijinx, The Sherman, Theatre West Glamorgan, Volcano, Y Cwmni. (And in so doing I in no way want to diminish the work of other companies like Arad Goch, Dalier Sylw, Magdalena Project and so on; this is a sample, not a selection.) I would like to avoid the debatable "metanarrative" that a whole can be made up of its parts, but let us say that one reason a National Theatre of Wales is unnecessary is because the different companies already operating themselves do culturally what a National Theatre would do: offer a product that is distinctively Welsh.

Take, for example, the Sherman Theatre Company, just the sort of organization that might seem to be modelled on the English-style building-based theatre company, and indeed was originally formed as a South Wales version of a national theatre company by a misguided Arts Council. It is true that it offers world theatre "classics", from *Ghosts* to *Romeo and Juliet*, but it

48

does a lot more and even when it does it usually seems to me to do so in quite a different way from an English building-based company. Under the artistic direction of Phil Clark, the Sherman is one manifestation of the tradition that has grown up since the birth of theatre in Wales in the 1960s, a tradition that puts accessibility high on its priorities and has community theatre at the core of its provision. Phil Clark says that his artistic policy would be the same wherever he was and that he doesn't have a "Welsh theatre" agenda. (In fact Clark is seen by some as guilty of stereotyping South Wales.) But by choosing plays that often resonate locally and by employing actors who frequently are involved in the Welsh debate, Clark (a Welshman whose professional roots are in community theatre) does, albeit inadvertently (he would say), produce what might be seen as a distinctively Welsh theatre. The form and style of mainstage productions tends to utilise the techniques of community theatre - populism, audience-friendliness, local actors: *A Taste of Honey*, for example, transferred its setting effortlessly from Salford to Cardiff and was staged much as a community show touring to village halls would have been - music-hall influenced, asides to the audience, musical accompaniment, local accents. It was, of course, a play that lent itself to the staging since Joan Littlewood came from the same place theatrically as community theatre. Market forces influence the Sherman's programming and *A Taste of Honey* was produced because it was a GCSE "set text"; but the Sherman also did it because their brief is to encourage young audiences. Clark also believes in encouraging new local writers and has spent a lot of time and energy trying to help Valleys playwright Frank Vickery make the qualitative leap from very funny but thin sitcoms to more meaningful comedies - with variable success. They have a thriving youth theatre that is bringing on new actors and writers. The company, while perhaps too often lacking excitement or robustness, is an integral part of the Welsh theatre scene with a policy of local casting, commissioning new writers and offering a stage to new companies. What National Theatre could do more? Clark's support of the National Theatre project is surprising and encouraging and, perhaps, means that if it should happen the Sherman Theatre Company could concentrate more on lower-key, developmental work and leave the obligatory classics to a big brother National Theatre Company.

If the Sherman Theatre Company has translated community-theatre values to the main stage, Wales's county-wide community theatre companies have raised the status of this much-belittled form of theatre to a remarkable level. In Wales community theatre companies are not seen as training-grounds for aspiring artists. They are, conversely, the bedrock of theatre provision and the theatrical skills of community-theatre practitioners are as valued as those in any other form, whether mainstream, experimental or television. Theatre West Glamorgan, for example, are constantly cited as a company capable of generating as much excitement, of creating as large an audience and of displaying as much excellence as any theatre anywhere. Set up, like Wales's other community companies, to service a population that had access to few large theatre buildings and little or no tradition of touring theatre, Theatre West Glamorgan has under Tim Baker developed a recognizable style of populist, often political, good-night-out musical entertainment. Like the other community companies, it also acts as a theatre-in-education service, a role it has refined to a fine art with videos, information packs and day workshops. The company is distinctly Welsh for a variety of reasons, at the root of which is the commitment to speaking to, challenging and engaging local audiences using local issues in local venues through the medium of theatre. If there is a criticism of the company, it is that its very professionalism is too slick to make their social criticisms hit home: with its well-crafted, cleverly-staged audience-friendly productions it creates a feel-good factor that more than sugars the satirical pill.

At the other extreme we have Volcano Theatre, a company whom many might consider only coincidentally Welsh. It is based in Swansea because the members met while at University there but it now tours far more extensively outside Wales than inside. How is a violent dramatization of Tony Harrison's controversial poem *V*, an unashamedly political exposition of Marx and Mayakovsky, *Manifesto*, a radical and sexually-charged interpretation of Shakespeare's sonnets, *L.O.V.E.* a controversial exploration of nihilism and postmodernism, especially the ideas of Nietzsche and Baudrillard, in *After the Orgy,* or a wickedly funny deconstruction of Ibsen, *How to Live*, anything to do with Wales or cultural identity? Volcano has never directly addressed issues of nationalism or Welshness and sees itself working in a culture that is in retreat and so "prefers the past to the present and the known to the unknown," in its view. Even so, the geographical and cultural location seems to me to be relevant. The company is different in style, form and content and challenges conventional theatre from a guerrilla base that is the stronger for being in an occupied territory. It would, I think, see itself as part of a dissident but popular Marxist movement that flourished in Wales. The aim is to take texts, often classics, and question them and their place in any supposed tradition - an artistic policy that is analogous to a political agenda that sees Wales as a culture that today does not sit easily in a capitalist world. Its connections have been with European cultures that relate to Wales more than England, like Catalonia and Macedonia. And, of course, Volcano is Welsh at least by definition of being based here: its Welshness means that although very popular and highly thought-of in London (it sold out at the South Bank) it is still not taken as seriously by English-based critics as if it were English. The company found it particularly ironic when recently it planned a radical production of *Under Milk Wood* with Welsh, Albanian and English actors under a Croatian director in Swansea, only to find it was denied the performing rights to the play because England's National Theatre was staging it in London. (Volcano still did it, staged for free, with no little irony, in a heritage centre on the Gower!)

In terms of sheer excitement there is (or was) only one Welsh company to match Volcano: Y Cwmni, formed specifically to produce the plays of writer Ed Thomas. With Brith Gof, it could only exist in present-day Wales because the nature and status of Welshness is what it is all about. Virtually everything Thomas writes addresses itself to the problem of cultural identity and he echoes Gwyn Alf's ideas about an invented Wales. His first major play, *House of America*, was a metaphor for Wales's reliance on myth and tradition, its low self-esteem, its apparent need to tell lies about itself, its dependence on American culture. It's an amazing piece of theatre, possibly the best play to have come out of Wales, and it speaks eloquently of the dilemma of the artist discovering that he has no tradition, no ready-made culture, no obvious identity. Thomas's plays continue to explore similar themes and he remains the one playwright to try to express a cultural identity that has to do away with a lot of baggage about nation and language - Thomas is a Welsh-speaker but has written only one play in Welsh. But the fact he has his own company is important, because part of his philosophy - and the crux of Y Cwmni - is that Welsh theatre has to find a new form and style. *House of America* may have been basically naturalistic (though Thomas's own direction subverted it) but little else has. His second full-length play, *Adar Heb Adenydd*, for Dalier Sylw, is his only Welsh-language play but was enough to make the point that he believes naturalism and Welsh to be incompatible. *The Myth of Michael Roderick*, more or less a translation, was an odd thing, a non-naturalistic play in English that challenged traditional ideas of Welshness but somehow felt too bizarre and needed to be in Welsh to have impact. *Flowers of the Dead Red Sea*, *East From the Gantry*, *Hiraeth* and *Song for a Forgotten City* continue the project to find a new voice: *East From the Gantry* in particular, it seems to me, released a lyricism in language, an expressionistic style and a provocative theme that dealt again with Wales's invisibility and lack of self-image. Where Thomas's pessimism will lead him I do not know, but he does articulate some of those elements I have already mentioned: the lack of profile, the lack of confidence, the rejection of romantic myths and the need to create new ones that, ironically, is perhaps just what Wales's cultural identity is at the moment. In rejecting a fabricated nationalistic culture and a lack of identity Thomas and Y Cwmni are contributing to Wales's cultural identity. Ironically, by the time this essay appears the company may well not exist, its enthusiastic bubble burst; but Ed Thomas will continue to write and direct and the likes of Russell Gomer and Richard Lynch will continue to act in his plays and the spirit of challenge and the debate about Welshness will go on.

What about Hijinx, different yet again? Clearly this company too has its roots in community theatre and much of its work is targeted at audiences with learning difficulties. No other company in Britain, I think, has taken on such a brief, but arguably Hijinx could be based anywhere. At first sight it is straining the notion of Welsh theatre as an expression of Welsh cultural identity to see Hijinx as offering a product that is a part of a discrete indigenous Welsh theatre, just as initially it was to see Volcano in that way. The work may be targeted at identifiable audiences (though usually definable only as "community") but it is produced with an attention to detail that can be quite astonishing - and results in a theatre product that is simply very high quality, as evidenced in the recent BBC Arts Award for the best company in Wales. In that year, for example, it toured four shows to around 6,500 people. One, Larry Allen's *On The Road Again*, included an actor with brittle bone disease and explored with humour, sensitivity and honesty the relationship between two of society's misfits; another, *Carpet of Dreams*, was a storytelling collaboration with Theatr Iolo and the company also toured a solo storytelling show; and *Ill Met by Moonlight* was a truly magical piece of theatre written by Charlie Way that combined music, romance and an unnostalgic look at the disappearance of rural folklore and customs in the border counties as modern life replaced the old ways. Each production had a rigour and performance quality that was impressive and each was highly accessible and challenging, entertaining and thoughtful.

The aim, they say, is to create celebratory theatre with universal themes, to take theatre to groups within the community for whom theatre is not easily accessible for whatever reason and to "encourage the integration of non-disabled and disabled people both as audience and participants in the creative process". It sounds noble; it actually makes for immensely moving theatre produced with great conviction - which is what you get if you mix commitment and skill. But identifiably Welsh? I think so, and not only because the company has chosen to be based in Wales, recruit locally and prioritise Welsh audiences - and manifest that *difference* in style, form and content. Hijinx expresses and reflects something that is very Welsh - a sense of community. Its whole ethos is about caring, co-operation, sharing, and it is expressed in everything the company does: not only in the performances, but in the company structure, its process of working, its commitment to touring, its specific concern for special groups. It is an awareness that is a reflection of social life in Wales, where the sense of community may be under threat but where the term does at least still have meaning and reality. Like Volcano, Hijinx would not, I think, suggest that it is at all concerned with Welshness but like Volcano, it is, it seems to me, very much a product of and an active contributor to a culture that is defined to some extent by its social and political values. It is the sort of symbiotic relationship that is rare and very special.

I have left Brith Gof to last in this trawl because the company itself proclaims that it produces "national theatre" - but not in the sense that a National Theatre of Wales would. If you speak to anyone outside Wales about Welsh theatre they will very soon mention Brith Gof: it is seen as the epitome of Welshness and of a distinct form of performance - a tribute to the company's own insistence that its aim "to create a new and alternative theatre discourse in Wales" was exclusively theirs. Small wonder that other practitioners resent Brith Gof's self-created high profile. Ironically, Brith Gof is English-led - and there are those in Welsh theatre that would accuse it of precisely the exercise of power that I mentioned right at the beginning of this essay: the colonialist's taking from an exotic culture, selecting from a position of dominance, making Wales an English invention, creating an artificial Wales.

Co-founder and director Mike Pearson is an articulate practitioner with an academic fertile mind, a performer who seemingly has to justify himself continually. Ten years ago, at a conference in Catalunya, he proclaimed: "The aim of Brith Gof is to develop a new, vibrant and distinctive theatre tradition in Wales, one which is relevant and responsive to the perceptions, experience, aspirations and concerns of a minority culture and a small nation and which is more than just a pale reflection of English theatre convention." The company's contribution to Welsh theatre may be as much, maybe more, to do with its theorizing as its practice, even more so since scenographer Cliff McLucas became co-director. Welsh theatre may be invisible but Brith Gof is not, at least in academic drama: in 1994/5 Pearson and/or Brith Gof were featured at great length in *The Drama Review*, the world's leading performance journal, *Contemporary Theatre Review*, the leading British theoretical publication, and *The New Welsh Review*; the company published *Y Llyfr Glas*, a glossy £6 book recording current directors McLucas and Pearson's latest thoughts; lecture/presentations on performance theory were given in half-a-dozen universities; three papers were presented in Cardiff, Amsterdam and Ljubljana. More recently, Pearson feels that the company has become a victim of its own success in Wales, with its innovative practices seen as commonplace; this may be true, but it is also that (thanks to some degree to Brith Gof) Welsh audiences are not impressed merely by innovation - as I have suggested, much Welsh theatre is defined by its difference, its rejection of naturalism and of mainstream theatre. And there are other, lower-profile, companies doing more innovative work.

I first saw Brith Gof at an off-field National Eisteddfod performance at Llanbedr Pont Steffan - *Rhydcymerau*, about afforestation and rural decay, staged in a cattle market. It was in Welsh (Mike Pearson, an English archaeology graduate of University College Cardiff, having learned Welsh after cofounding Cardiff Laboratory Theatre in 1973) but nevertheless for me had an urgency, an excitement and a freshness that signified a major new theatrical presence in Wales. John Berger's *Boris*, staged in December 1985 in a barn at St Fagan's Folk Museum with the audience on straw bales and with sheep, was also stunning. I found *Pandemonium: The True Cost of Coal*, a co-production with Theatr Taliesin Wales in Morriston's Tabernacl Chapel in 1987, disappointing - and perhaps a hint of that element of trite political statement that for me marred later works. The ambitious three-year *Disasters of War* project, based on Goya's etchings, culminated in *Gododdin*, to my mind their best production, in 1988/9. It was a period of amazing creative energy, of collaborations and of development, and it was, perhaps, the date from which we can date the birth of a distinctive Welsh theatre outside the Welsh language. Coincidentally, Moving Being under Geoff Moore, by then based at St Stephen's Theatre Space in Cardiff docklands, were staging works that in content, style and form (and, crucially, in performers) offered a theatre that was different - *In These Great Times* (where we were customers at a Viennese café), *The Rising*, *In Dusseldorf and Nebraska*, a Shakespeare season which offered directors Hugh Thomas, Jamie Garven, Ceri Sherlock and Moore the chance to create fresh interpretations of classics, and a "radical writing" season that included Moore's production of Howard Barker's *No End of Blame* - and Ed Thomas's *House of America*, which saw the birth of Y Cwmni; St Stephen's also became the nursery for Dalier Sylw. Volcano burst onto the scene with *Greek*, *Tell-Tale Heart*, *Magbeth* and *V*. At the same time Theatre West Glamorgan in *You Me and the Gatepost,* for example, were showing that community theatre did not have to be safe or didactic with accessible, slick, immaculately-done musicals about urgent local issues.

Since *The Disasters of War* Brith Gof's performance work has had mixed reactions as its theoretical output increasingly impresses. *Pax*, which was performed in St David's Hall and Aberystwyth railway station, among other venues, in 1990/91, I enjoyed enormously but many found it empty. *Patagonia* had many interesting qualities, not least its use of a deceptively simple set and the creation of the idea of open spaces, its multilayered content and its exploration of "hyperreality", with the classic opening line "Maybe Baudrillard was right..." - and the first obvious evidence that Mike Pearson was letting contemporary thinking set the agenda of the company's theatre work. *Haearn*, a complex multimedia extravaganza staged in a disused Tredegar coalworks, impressed through its ambition, its parallel themes of dehumanizing industrialization, the Frankenstein story, the Prometheus v Hephaestus myth, the development of eighteenth-century science and medicine, and the sheer pyrotechnics of the event. Their *Arturius Rex* project divided audiences: some were greatly moved, others found it simplistic, poorly realized and repetitive and such conflicting responses to the company's work have started a debate about the nature of postmodernist theatre and its ability to address cultural and political issues. I should admit, perhaps, that personally, while I do not think I have any problems coming to terms critically with a theatre that rejects conventional theatre spaces, that places the audience in the "action", that denies authoritative meaning, that accuses the audience of complicity, that uses discontinuity, ambiguity and ambivalence, I simply did not engage with productions like *Camlann*, *DOA* or *Arturius Rex,* partly because in addressing the Bosnian war they seem to me transparent, clichéd, trite.

But Brith Gof are important, of course, even if it seems less innovative to others than it sees itself, and if only because of the theorizing they have contributed to the debate about defining "Welsh theatre". When they insist that theatre is "a place where identities - personal, artistic, national - are actually created, contested and altered and not just reflected or represented," many of us would agree. And their practice has helped change theatre in Wales - along with other companies'.

All these companies - and the other fifty or so that work in Wales - seem to me to constitute a kind of national theatre.

While we may detect the broken line of an invisible indigenous folk drama, the absence of an obvious long theatrical tradition has been used to advantage, since there is no need to fight an entrenched convention like naturalism. The youthfulness means there is no real homogeneity. The challenges of cultural domination have led to experiments in form, in style, in content and in language, theatre being at the forefront of the search for a distinctive voice both linguistically and politically.

What would a National Theatre - in terms of a company, a building, an institution and an idea - contribute? Welsh theatre's weakness (if an absence has to be seen as a weakness) is in larger-scale English-language scripted work, what's usually called mainstage or mainstream or literary theatre: Theatr Clwyd is now (since the demise of the Torch company and the emphasis on young people's theatre and the community style of the Sherman) the only major company producing such work, and it is frequently charged with being more English than Welsh. It means that writers like Greg Cullen, Dic Edwards, Siôn Eirian, Peter Lloyd, Ed Thomas and Charlie Way (to name the handful of established writers working at least in part in English in Wales) may sometimes have to take their larger-scale plays to television, film or England to be produced - although all also write for smaller Welsh stages, in Thomas's case a company set up exclusively to produce his plays, and several are already turning to non-professional (that is, community and youth) theatre projects where large-scale plays can be staged. It means that the few plays by earlier Welsh playwrights (Gwyn Thomas and Emlyn Williams, for instance) will rarely be staged.

But I think that this "mainstage" work is to an extent alien to Wales and I, for one, am quite happy to let those cultures which have developed strengths in such theatre forms perform them - let the RSC and National Theatre bring their "mainstage" works to Wales, to any new Cardiff Bay theatre, to The New and other larger houses, and share the fruits of centuries of that dramatic tradition. Wales, if it has confidence in its own cultural integrity and difference, should be strong enough to welcome such shows as examples of an English cultural product. First, though, maybe Wales should take some pride in its own discrete, heterogeneous, vibrant performance. Investing in an artificial institution like a National Theatre may not be to the advantage of today's living Welsh theatre.

EPILOGUE

It is the year 2006. The National Theatre Company of Wales's spring season is announced: in the main auditorium of the Cardiff Bay Lyric Theatre a retrospective of the work of Welsh-born playwright Dic Edwards, including early works like *Casanova Undone* and *Wittgenstein's Daughter*, amazingly never performed in Wales; the latest work by Gareth Miles, directed by Bethan Jones, a savage attack on the stranglehold of New Labour on the Welsh Assembly, performed in Welsh with surtitles; the Black Workshop's devised musical based on the 1998 race riots; at NTW Theatr Clwyd the company will be performing these and a joint production with NTW Theatre of Bangor, formerly Theatr Gwynedd, of a "contemporary mythic pageant" directed by Ceri Sherlock. In the studio space Mike Pearson, founder of the legendary and fondly-remembered Brith Gof, presents his latest one-man show; Theatr y Byd's performance-installation is premiered before going to the Sydney Festival; the clutch of new directors to emerge from the NTCW's training scheme in Swansea and Bangor showcase their talents with "classic" Welsh plays of the last century from W.J. Gruffydd, Caradoc Evans, Saunders Lewis, John Gwilym Jones, Gwenlyn Parry, Gwyn Thomas and Peter Gill; Jeremy Turner is directing his latest production in the series of "reclaimed" Welsh indigenous drama, timed to coincide with the complete reorganization of the National Gallery that sees work by Welsh artists, arranged and contextualised, replace the old museum's collection of foreign masterpieces (now exhibited on a rotation basis in a special "European Tradition" room). Michael Bogdanov, the NTW artistic director, continues his "Heritage" initiative with a *Drovers Project* to be performed in and around Carmarthen market place and sponsored by the Ministry of Agriculture, Food and Fisheries and Macdonalds (whose logo has been inverted to form a Big W for Wales).

Elsewhere the *International Festival of Young People's Theatre* will have performances in the NTW's three YPT centres in

Aberystwyth, Mold and Cardiff and the English National Theatre continues the Foreign Visitors season with a residency at NTW Wrexham. The national theatres of Canada, South Africa, Australia and Ireland will be at NTW Swansea for the "alien english" festival.

The events are expected to receive intensive media coverage.

Meanwhile the Welsh Independent Theatre Umbrella plans an "alternative" festival where existing members of former companies will re-create the spirit of such pre-millenium groups as Y Cwmni, Dalier Sylw, Hijinx, Moving Being and Mappa Mundi, when it also hopes that Alma, Man Act, Volcano Theatre and other companies now based in Europe will return for the extravaganza.

FOOTNOTE

If this essay were not a piece of journalism but an academic article, there would be lots of footnotes acknowledging published sources of information and scholarship. These would include works by Jane Aaron, Benedict Anderson, Bill Ashcroft, Gareth Griffiths and Helen Tiffin, Linda Colley, Jacques Derrida, Trevor Fishlock, Michel Foucault, Wyn Griffith, Glyn Jones, Jacques Lacan, Peter Lord, Tom Maguire, Kenneth O. Morgan, Prys Morgan, John Osmond, Thomas Parry, Patrice Pavis, Mike Pearson, Cecil Price, Edward Said, Dai Smith, Elan Closs Stephens, Meic Stephens, R. S. Thomas, A. Watkin-Jones, Charlotte Williams, Gwyn A. Williams and others, sometimes shamelessly used without credit, in true postmodernist style. However, as a piece of journalism it draws on the research and ideas of those authorities mentioned and also on many personal conversations over the past fifteen years or so and especially more recently with Gilly Adams, Mike Baker, Michael Bogdanov, Phil Clark, Greg Cullen, Dic Edwards, Steve Fletcher, Geoff Moore, Ed Thomas, Jeremy Turner, Charlie Way, Yvette Vaughan Williams, Hazel Walford Davies and many other professional theatre practitioners in Wales whom I respect more than they can ever know.

David Adams, October 1995